Impact on Earth

The Impact of

THE INTERNET

Tim Cooke

Crabtree Publishing Company
www.crabtreebooks.com

CRABTREE
PUBLISHING COMPANY
WWW.CRABTREEBOOKS.COM

Author: Tim Cooke

Editorial director: Kathy Middleton

Editor: Ellen Rodger

Picture Manager: Sophie Mortimer

Design Manager: Keith Davis

Children's Publisher: Anne O'Daly

Production coordinator and prepress: Ken Wright

Print coordinator: Katherine Berti

Photo credits
(t=top, b= bottom, l=left, r=right, c=center)

Front Cover: Shutterstock / Shawn Hempel tl; All other images from Shutterstock

Interior: Shutterstock: 24Novembers 17, Africa Studio 23, Mark Agnor 25, Tero Besalainen 15, bluebay 5, Chinnapong 18, Sam DCruz 9, Dotted Yeti 27, Iakov Filimonov 28, G-Stock Sutdio 6, Aleksandr Khakimullin 19, metamorworks 26, Monkey Business Images 14, 29, NicoElNino 24, Sura Nualpradid 20, oculo 11, Mark Oleksiy 4, Andrey Popov 12, Rawpixel.com 16, SeventyFour 22, Bernhard Staehli 10, stickypedro 8, Winai Tepsuttinun 21, Jonathan Weiss 7, Marcus Mesa Sam Wordley 13.

Library and Archives Canada Cataloguing in Publication

Title: The impact of the Internet / Tim Cooke.
Names: Cooke, Tim, 1961- author.
Description: Series statement: Impact on Earth | Includes index.
Identifiers: Canadiana (print) 20190236698 |
Canadiana (ebook) 20190236701 |
ISBN 9780778774389 (hardcover) |
ISBN 9780778774839 (softcover) |
ISBN 9781427125170 (HTML)
Subjects: LCSH: Digital communications—Environmental aspects—Juvenile literature. | LCSH: Digital communications—Social aspects—Juvenile literature. | LCSH: Telecommunication—Environmental aspects—Juvenile literature. |
LCSH: Telecommunication—Social aspects—Juvenile literature. |
LCSH: Internet—Social aspects—Juvenile literature.
Classification: LCC TK5102.4 .C66 2020 | DDC j621.382—dc23

Library of Congress Cataloging-in-Publication Data

Names: Cooke, Tim, 1961- author.
Title: The impact of the internet / Tim Cooke.
Description: New York, NY : Crabtree Publishing Company, 2020. |
Series: Impact on Earth |
Includes bibliographical references and index.
Identifiers: LCCN 2019053359 (print) | LCCN 2019053360 (ebook)
ISBN 9780778774389 (hardcover) |
ISBN 9780778774839 (paperback) |
ISBN 9781427125170 (ebook)
Subjects: LCSH: Internet--Social aspects--Juvenile literature. |
Electronic industries--Environmental aspects--Juvenile literature.
| Human ecology--Juvenile literature.
Classification: LCC HM851 .C67455 2020 (print) |
LCC HM851 (ebook) | DDC 302.23/1--dc23
LC record available at https://lccn.loc.gov/2019053359
LC ebook record available at https://lccn.loc.gov/2019053360

Published in 2020 by Crabtree Publishing Company

All rights reserved. No part of this publication may be reproduced, stored in a retrieval system or be transmitted in any form or by any means, electronic, mechanical, photocopying, recording, or otherwise, without the prior written permission of the copyright owner.

Copyright © Brown Bear Books Ltd. 2020
Brown Bear Books has made every attempt to contact the copyright holder. If you have any information about omissions, please contact licensing@brownbearbooks.co.uk.

Printed in the U.S.A./022020/CG20200102

Published in Canada
Crabtree Publishing
616 Welland Avenue
St. Catharines, ON
L2M 5V6

Published in the United States
Crabtree Publishing
PMB 59051
350 Fifth Ave, 59th Floor
New York, NY 10118

Contents

What Is the Internet? 4

What's the Problem? 8

Social Media 12

Fake News 16

Reducing the Harm 20

Future Developments 24

Your Turn! 28

Glossary 30

Find Out More 31

Index 32

What Is the Internet?

The Internet joins together computers all over the world. Since it was invented in 1983, it has changed life in many ways.

The Internet is a network, or connected group, of computers around the world. People use it to communicate by email or **social media**. Social media such as Facebook or Instagram allows people to post messages or images for other people to see.

All the information on the Internet is stored on machines called servers. Servers are sometimes grouped together in large collections.

TECHNOLOGY SOLUTIONS

Cloud Computing

There is a huge amount of **data** on the Internet. There is too much to be stored on the computers people use at home or at work. Instead, this information is stored in what is called "the cloud." The cloud is really made up of millions of **servers**. Servers fill whole rooms and use a lot of electricity.

About 80 million

Number of servers around the world in 2018

Environmental Impact

People use the Internet through devices such as tablets and smartphones, as well as computers. These devices use electricity. Most electricity is made by burning coal or oil. This releases **greenhouse gases** that trap heat near Earth, warming the planet. This is having a major impact on Earth.

Many people use the Internet to work at home. They can see the same files as if they were in their office, talk to other people, and even attend meetings by video.

Communications Revolution

The Internet allows people to watch videos or listen to songs, or to hold video calls with their friends and family. It is useful for research for students writing reports. It also has wider effects on the way we live. For example, many companies now allow people to work from home. Employees use the Internet to stay in touch with the office. They can spend less time traveling to work and more time with family.

Changing Business

Some people have started new types of businesses. They sell goods or services online to customers around the world. Many shoppers use the Internet to order goods. The goods arrive by mail. Fewer visitors go to downtown shopping districts and malls. This has reduced the number of shoppers in stores.

About 3 million Number of packages Amazon ships each day

About 12 million Number of packages Alibaba, a similar website in China, ships each day

· EMERGENCY · EMERGENCY ·

Amazon

Amazon is one of the largest companies in the world. It was one of the first online retailers. It began selling books in 1994 and grew to sell other goods, too. Many people prefer to buy online than travel to shop in stores. It can often be cheaper and more convenient. The result is that fewer people visit malls, and stores close down.

What's the Problem?

The Internet improves our lives in many ways. However, it also has a negative impact, both on Earth and on individuals.

Computers use electricity. A lot of electricity is made by burning **fossil fuels**, such as coal and oil. Fossil fuels were formed inside Earth millions of years ago. They are non-renewable, which means they cannot be replaced when they run out. In addition, computers and other devices contain many **minerals** from Earth's crust, which are also non-renewable.

Burning coal and oil at power plants releases gases and pollution harmful to the environment. These gases contribute to the increase in Earth's temperature.

EMERGENCY· EMERGENCY·

Funding War

Computers, smartphones, and tablets contain rare materials, such as tungsten. The minerals are found underground. In Africa, these minerals are mined in the Democratic Republic of Congo. **Armed rebels** there fight the government to control the mines. They sell the minerals to get money for weapons and supplies. The fighting has forced many people to flee their homes.

62 **Number of different minerals contained in an average smartphone**

2.7 billion **Number of smartphone users worldwide**

Doing Harm to Individuals

Unfortunately, the Internet can be used to cause harm to others. It is easy to spread false information and lies, or to bully people. Criminals also use the Internet to steal money. Not everyone has access to the Internet either. They can't take advantage of the same knowledge or services as people who do.

Getting Warmer

About 3.5 billion people around the world use computers. So many devices using electricity are taking a toll. Burning fossil fuels to create the **energy** computers use releases the greenhouse gas **carbon dioxide**. This gets trapped in the **atmosphere** surrounding Earth. It stops the Sun's rays from bouncing off the planet and back into space. The result is a planet that is getting warmer.

As the atmosphere gets warmer, the ice at Earth's north and south poles melts. The melting ice causes sea levels to rise. This leads to flooding in low-lying countries.

TECHNOLOGY SOLUTIONS

Spam

Emails created by machines and sent to random email addresses are called spam. Spam emails are usually used to try to sell you a product or service. Every day, 14 billion spam emails are sent, releasing a tiny amount of carbon dioxide with each one. Computer **programs** are being designed to try to spot spam to prevent it from being delivered.

12.5 million **Average number of messages a spammer must send to get one response**

Cutting Carbon

Making and using computers and servers burns energy. The Internet creates about 3 percent of Earth's greenhouse gases. Internet use is still growing. Within 50 years, the Internet may create up to 8 percent of greenhouse gases. This will harm efforts to reduce how much **carbon** is released into the atmosphere.

Social Media

Many people use social media to keep in touch with their family and friends. However, social media can also have harmful effects.

Some people become addicted to checking social media and other online activities. Some people use social media to bully others. They might tease people or share embarrassing photos or information about them. Material like this can be shared among many people very quickly.

For most people, social media is a great way to find out what their friends are up to and send messages to one another. For others, it can cause distress.

EMERGENCY· EMERGENCY·

Signs of Addiction

About six percent of Internet users become addicted. People spend so long online that it affects their day-to-day lives. This is especially true for teenagers and children. Placing time limits on Internet use and encouraging sports and exercise are ways to lessen online addiction.

7 hours Average number of hours spent online every day by children ages 8 to 18

2 hours Maximum number of hours experts recommend

Being Mean

Online bullying can make a person feel like everyone is laughing at them. In person, people are usually careful not to act like bullies because others will disapprove. It is easier online to keep your identity secret. Being anonymous can make people feel like they can behave in harmful or unkind ways that they never would in person.

One result of online bullying is that it makes the victim feel alone. They might feel that everyone else is laughing at them.

Cyberbullying

Bullying online is called **cyberbullying**. The person being bullied may not even know who the bully is. People bully other people openly on social media for anyone to see, or in private text messages or emails. It is easy for somone to put stories or photographs online, and much harder for someone else to remove them.

Feeling Alone

Victims of cyberbullying often feel alone. It might seem to them that everyone wants to hurt them, not just one person. Often, bullies do not understand the full effect bullying has on the victim. Anyone who is being cyberbullied should tell an adult, such as a teacher or parent. Schools and parents can take effective action to identify cyberbullies and stop them.

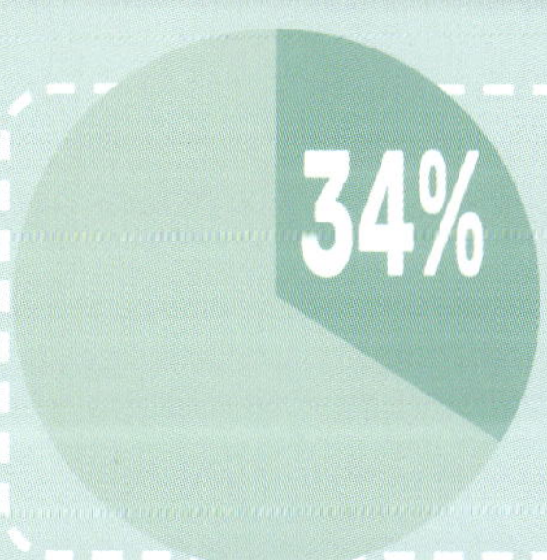

About 34% **Percentage of children in U.S.A. who say they have been cyberbullied**

About 17% **Percentage of children in Canada**

TECHNOLOGY SOLUTIONS

Computer Defense

Apps are being developed that will search social media posts and texts for negative keywords that are often used by bullies. Other programs search for people who have been bullied. They look for phrases that show someone is very upset. The goal is to catch abuse early and stop it.

Fake News

Fake news is a name given to information that sounds true but is not. The Internet makes it easy for fake news to spread.

One example of misinformation that went **viral** was a study that declared childhood **vaccinations** cause **autism**. Fearful parents did not get their children vaccinated. After the study's authors were found to have made up facts, the study was exposed as a **fraud**. However, some people continue to believe this false story today, showing just how hard it is to correct false information once it's out there.

Sticking to newspapers and media that check facts makes it easier to avoid being tricked by fake news.

EMERGENCY· EMERGENCY·

Climate Change

Almost all scientific experts agree climate change is made worse by human activity, such as burning fossil fuels. However, some people do not accept the scientific evidence because of their religious or political views. Information based on facts is often difficult to separate from information based on **opinions** on the Internet.

70% **Percentage that fake news stories are more likely to be retweeted than accurate news stories on Twitter**

52% **Percentage of adults in U.S.A. who get their news from Facebook**

Reliable Information

Facts are checked in most newspapers and media, but many Internet sites do not check their stories. Anyone can write an opinion and publish it online. Their ideas are often not checked or challenged. Other people may read the stories and believe the information to be fact.

Safety Online

Some basic tips will keep you safe online. The best way to stay safe is not to give out personal information. If you are contacted by strangers, do not tell them your name or where you live. Do not open emails from people you do not know unless you are expecting a message. Do not post public photos of yourself or your friends. Set your social media so that only your friends can see your posts.

Many people spend private time online. A good rule to follow is never to share personal information with other people you are in contact with online.

WHAT CAN I DO?

Check It Out

Protect yourself against fake news by looking to see who created a story. Look for the names of broadcasters or newspapers you recognize. Check to see if the author is a regular writer. Do not trust just one account of a story. Use other websites to see whether all sources agree.

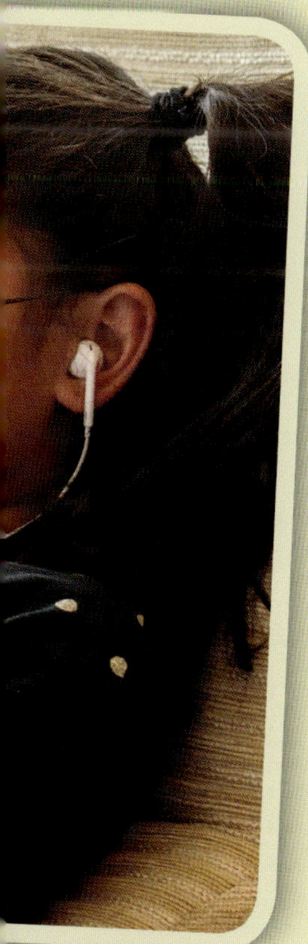

554 **Average number of friends on social media, from a poll in Britain**

5 **Average number of close friends in real life reported by same people in poll**

Take Action

If a stranger starts sending you messages, tell an adult, such as a parent or teacher. Show them any communications you get. Do not respond to requests for personal information or send images. Stick to websites that you know and trust. These might include sites run by news organizations or well-known businesses.

Reducing the Harm

Many people are trying to reduce the negative impact of the Internet, both to the planet and to individual users.

Companies are building computers that use less energy. Other firms are making other changes. Ecosia is a search engine for finding information online. It promises to plant trees as people join its service.

Trees absorb carbon dioxide from the air, reducing the amount held in the atmosphere. Trees also give off oxygen, a gas necessary to nearly all life on Earth.

TECHNOLOGY SOLUTIONS

Reconditioning Devices

One way to cut the amount of energy related to Internet use is to reduce the number of new computers and other devices we make that run on electricity. Some old tablets, computers, and smartphones can be **reconditioned**. That means up-to-date parts and more memory are added. Less plastic and minerals are used than in making new devices.

20 times more energy can be saved by using a reconditioned computer instead of recycling the plastic and other materials in it

Reducing Server Energy

Internet companies are trying to use less energy. They store information in huge data centers. These centers use up to 70 percent less energy than normal servers. This cuts the amount of carbon that is released into the air. The energy they use comes from **renewable** sources, such as wind power or energy from the Sun.

Keeping Cool

Servers are computers that store data on disks. As the disks spin, they create heat which could destroy the data. Servers must be cooled by fans or water-cooling systems. This uses a lot of electricity. Data centers use a system called hyperscale technology, in which many servers are grouped together. Some companies are experimenting with renewable energy sources such as wind and solar power for their data centers. Others are trying to make the servers' waste heat usable as energy to heat homes.

Hyperscale servers can spread the work the computers are doing across different servers, so that no individual server gets too hot. This way, they stay much cooler than regular servers.

WHAT CAN I DO?

Reducing the Power

You can cut down your own online energy use. Turn off your computer or other devices when you are not using them. Once they are fully charged, unplug them. Keep your files tidy! Storing information uses energy, so keep only one copy of each file and delete old files.

6.4 million **Number of average homes whose total energy use equalled the total energy used by servers in data centers in U.S.A. in 2016**

Powering Down

Servers are not busy all the time. Late at night, for example, fewer people are online. Facebook has a new system called Autoscale. It reacts to how many people are using Facebook's servers around the world. At slow times, it turns off servers to save energy.

Future Developments

We will only become more dependent on the Internet in our daily lives. Computers will be doing more with less human input.

Our homes and workplaces will be controlled by a system of connected devices giving instructions to each other using the Internet. This is called the Internet of Things. It means a "smart" refrigerator will be able to detect when milk is running low and order more milk itself from an online store.

The Internet of Things may eventually connect homes, workplaces, transportation, and stores in one huge network.

EMERGENCY· EMERGENCY· EM

Bitcoin

Bitcoin is a type of online money. Users can earn bitcoins by "mining," or running servers. This uses lots of energy. There are other **currencies** like Bitcoin. If they become popular, they will need huge servers. Keeping up with the demand for Internet currencies will be a big challenge in the future.

21 million Total number of Bitcoins that exist to be mined

About 1,800 Total number of new Bitcoins being mined each day

Cutting Energy Use

The increased use of the Internet will use more energy. However, the Internet of Things may help homes use less energy. Lights would be able to switch themselves off in empty rooms. Devices could automatically turn down heating if no one is at home.

One day you might be able to control activities in your home from your fridge! This could help you reduce your home's energy use.

Future Internet

Some experts think we are not far away from being online all of the time. We already use the Internet to find information and send messages. We also use it to stream movies and TV and listen to music. We use it to do our shopping, and we're beginning to use it to run our homes. The Internet will be vital for organizing our lives. This means there will be more demand for energy to power computers, servers, and smart devices. Scientists are trying to figure out where that energy will come from.

Making Changes

The answer might be a combination of changes. New types of computers and servers might use less energy. New sources of renewable energy might be developed to replace fossil fuels. Computers could make other devices more efficient. This might help save even more energy than the computers themselves use.

24 minutes

Amount of time it would take an Internet signal sent from Earth to reach Mars and back again

TECHNOLOGY SOLUTIONS

The Internet in Space

One day, the Internet may work beyond Earth. Humans are planning to explore other planets. If we do, scientists will find a way to beam powerful radio signals into space. Explorers on planets such as Mars will use the signals to go online. They will be able to use the Internet to communicate with Earth, get news, and find entertainment.

Your Turn!

How much energy do you use when you are online? Could you reduce it?

Gathering Evidence

Track how much time you spend online. Make a page in a notepad for each of your devices and divide each page into two columns. In the first column, write down all the time you are on each device over three days. In the second column, write down the time your devices are in standby or sleep mode.

- After three days, add up the total number of minutes you spent on each device, then add them together to get your full total. Divide the total by three to get an average length of time per day spent on devices.

Get offline and get outdoors! Make a plan to meet your friends rather than communicating with them online.

Using a smaller device, such as a tablet, rather than a computer will cut down the energy you use online.

Results

Energy use is measured in Watts. A desktop computer uses about 200 Watts per hour. A laptop uses between 50 and 100 Watts per hour. A smartphone uses about 5 Watts per hour. Use these numbers to figure out how many Watts you use each day for just these devices.

Finding Solutions

Can you think of changes that might help you cut your online energy use? One way is to put your devices in standby or sleep mode when you are not using them. This uses only about a third of normal power. If you turn them off completely, they use no power.

Glossary

apps Software programs

armed rebels People who use weapons to fight against their government

atmosphere The layers of gases that surround Earth

autism Conditions that can affect communication

carbon A chemical substance present in all living things

carbon dioxide A gas found naturally in the atmosphere, which is also produced when living things exhale and fossil fuels are burned

currencies Types of money used in particular places

cyberbullying Bullying that takes place online

data Information

energy Power used to do work

fossil fuels Fuels formed from the remains of things that lived millions of years ago

fraud Something designed with the intention to mislead

greenhouse gases Gases such as carbon dioxide that build up in the atmosphere and trap heat

minerals Useful substances that occur naturally in Earth

opinions Viewpoints that are beliefs which may or may not be supported by facts

programs Sets of instructions for computers

reconditioned Repaired so a thing works like new

renewable Able to be replaced rather than running out completely

servers Computers that store information

service providers Companies that give people access to the Internet

social media Applications that allow users to share messages and pictures

vaccinations Treatments that help the body fight disease

viral Viewed and shared quickly among many people

Find out More

Books

Dakers, Diane. *Information Literacy and Fake News (Why Does Media Literacy Matter?)*. Crabtree Publishing, 2018.

Grunbraum, Mara. *The Greenhouse Effect (Understanding Climate Change)*. Children's Press, 2020.

Hubbard, Ben. *My Digital Safety and Security (Digital Citizens)*. Lerner Publications, 2019.

Vink, Amanda. *The Dangers of Digital Addiction (Hot Topics)*. Lucent Press, 2019.

Websites

Visit this website to find out about climate change and the greenhouse effect.
climatekids.nasa.gov/greenhouse-effect/

This website has a lot of information about how web servers work.
computer.howstuffworks.com/web-server.htm

This video shows how to spot fake news.
www.commonsense.org/education/asset/video/video-how-to-spot-fake-news

Index

A B C D

addiction 12, 13
Amazon 7
atmosphere 10
Bitcoin 25
bullying 9, 12, 13, 14, 15
carbon dioxide 10, 11, 20, 21
climate change 8, 10
cloud, the 5
computers 4, 5, 8, 21, 27, 28, 29
cyberbullying 14, 15
data centers 21, 22
Democratic Republic of Congo 9

E F G I

Ecosia 20
email 4, 11
energy use 5, 8, 10, 20, 21, 22, 25, 26, 28–29
fake news 9, 16, 17, 19
fossil fuels 5, 8, 10, 27
greenhouse gases 10, 11
Internet of Things 24, 25

M N O

minerals 8, 9, 21
money 24, 25
newspapers 16, 17
online safety 18, 19

R S

reconditioning 21
renewable energy 21
safety online 18, 19
sea levels 10
servers 4, 5, 22, 23, 27
shopping 7
smart machines 24, 25
smartphones 5, 9, 21
social media 4, 12, 15
space exploration 27
spam 11

T V W

Twitter 17
vaccinations 16
wars 9
work 6, 7